Chapter 1: Once Upon a Time in California: Meet Katheryn Hudson

Once upon a time, in the sunny state of California, a future pop superstar was born! Katheryn Elizabeth Hudson, who the world would later know as Katy Perry, arrived on October 25, 1984, in a place called Santa Barbara. Imagine warm beaches, palm trees, and a little girl with a big voice just waiting to be heard!

Katheryn, or Katy as we'll call her, grew up in a very religious family. Her parents, Mary Christine (whose maiden name was Perry – that's a hint for later!) and Maurice Keith Hudson, were both pastors.

INTRODUCTION

Who is Katty Perry?

About Her

Katy Perry is a world-famous singer, songwriter, and performer known for her fun music, colorful outfits, and exciting concerts! She was born on October 25, 1984, in California, USA, and started singing in church when she was just a little girl.

Katy became a superstar with her hit song "I Kissed a Girl" in 2008, and later wowed the world with songs like "Firework," "Roar," and "Dark Horse." She's known for her powerful voice, catchy tunes, and positive messages that make people feel happy and confident.

Katy Perry also cares about helping others. She supports children's causes, helps fight hunger, and was even a judge on American Idol, helping new singers chase their dreams.

Katy shows kids that being creative, staying true to yourself, and spreading kindness can light up the world—just like a firework!

Pastors are like religious teachers who lead church services. Katy wasn't an only child; she had an older sister named Angela and a younger brother named David, who also grew up to be a singer! Because her parents set up new churches in different places, Katy's family moved around a lot when she was little, from when she was three until she was about eleven.

It was like having many mini-adventures across the country before they settled back in Santa Barbara.

Life in the Hudson household was quite strict. Since her parents were pastors, they had many rules. For example, Katy and her siblings mostly listened to gospel music, which is religious music. Other kinds of music, called secular music (like the pop songs we hear on the radio), were usually not allowed. There were even funny food rules! They weren't allowed to eat a cereal called Lucky Charms because the word "luck" reminded her mom of a scary figure called Lucifer.

And get this – they had to call "deviled eggs" (a type of egg dish) "ANGELED eggs" so they wouldn't use a word that sounded "bad"! These unique rules certainly made her childhood different. Sometimes, her family didn't have a lot of money, and they had to use food stamps or get food from food banks, which are places that help families who need it. Facing these challenges early on likely helped Katy become strong and determined.

Even though pop music wasn't played much at home, Katy was curious! She discovered it by secretly borrowing CDs from her friends. It must have felt like finding a hidden treasure! One day, a friend played a song called "You Oughta Know" by a singer named Alanis Morissette. Hearing that song was a huge moment for Katy; it really inspired her and made her think about the kind of music she wanted to make. The fact that this music was somewhat "forbidden" probably made it even more exciting and special to her, sparking a deep interest that would later shape her entire career.

Katy started singing very early, inspired by her older sister, Angela. She would practice with Angela's cassette tapes and then perform for her parents. They saw her talent and let her take vocal lessons, just like her sister. From the age of nine until she was seventeen, Katy sang in her parents' church. When she was thirteen, she got her very first guitar for her birthday! That's when she started writing her own songs and performing them for people.

Even with her religious upbringing, Katy was also a "typical Californian girl." She loved rollerskating, skateboarding, and even surfing! Her brother David said she was a bit of a "tomboy" when she was growing up, meaning she liked doing active, adventurous things. She also learned cool dances like the swing, Lindy Hop, and jitterbug. All these varied experiences – the moving, the strict rules, the secret discovery of pop music, her early performances, and her adventurous spirit – were like little seeds being planted, helping to grow the determined and unique superstar she would become.

Chapter 2: Nashville Dreams and LA Bound: The Long Road to "Katy Perry"

After discovering her love for music and performing, young Katy Hudson knew she wanted to be a singer. Her journey took her first to Nashville, Tennessee, a city famous for music, especially country and Christian music. Rock artists Steve Thomas and Jennifer Knapp heard her sing and brought her there to help her get better at writing songs and to record some demo tracks, which are like practice songs.

In Nashville, Katy signed with a record label called Red Hill Records. In 2001, when she was just 16, she released her very first album. It was a gospel album, fitting with her religious background, and it was titled Katy Hudson, using her real name. She even went on tour to perform her songs. However, the album didn't sell very many copies – maybe only a couple of hundred – and soon after, the record label went out of business. For many people, this might have been a sign to give up, but not for Katy!

This early experience, while not a big success, was actually a very important step. It taught her about the music world and pushed her to think about what kind of artist she truly wanted to be.

So, at the young age of 17, Katy made a big decision. She packed her bags and moved to Los Angeles, the heart of the pop music world, to try making secular (non-religious) music. This is also when she decided to change her stage name. To avoid being confused with the famous actress Kate Hudson, she started using her mother's maiden name, Perry. And just like that, Katheryn Hudson began her journey to becoming Katy Perry! This name change was a big step in creating her new pop star identity.

But becoming a pop star wasn't easy; in fact, it was a very long and often difficult road. For about five years, Katy faced many challenges in Los Angeles. She would get signed by record labels, like Java Records and later Columbia Records, only to be dropped, meaning they decided not to work with her anymore. She even recorded a whole album for Columbia called Fingerprints, but it was never released.

Another album she worked on with a production team called The Matrix also ended up being shelved, meaning it wasn't released either.

During these tough times, Katy struggled with money. She once said it was "five years of living in L.A. with no money, writing bad checks, selling my clothes to make rent, [and] borrowing money". Imagine having to sell your favorite clothes just to pay for your apartment! These years of hardship, filled with so many "no's" and disappointments, could have made anyone quit. But for Katy, each closed door seemed to make her more determined to find an open one.

She kept writing songs, performing in small clubs, and never gave up on her dream.

Along the way, there were little sparks of hope. One of her songs, called "Simple," was chosen to be in the movie The Sisterhood of the Traveling Pants in 2005. She also sang backup vocals for famous musicians like Mick Jagger (from The Rolling Stones) and the band P.O.D.. These small successes were like little reminders to keep going, proving that her talent was real and that her big break might be just around the corner.

Fun Fact: Before she was a superstar, Katy Perry had a song called "Simple" in the movie The Sisterhood of the Traveling Pants!.

Chapter 3:
"I Kissed a Girl" and a Star is Born!

After years of trying, working hard, and never giving up, Katy Perry's big moment finally arrived! In 2007, she signed a record deal with a major label called Capitol Records. This time, things were going to be different. The record label saw her potential and wanted to help her create a "splashy, chart-topping hit" that would make everyone take notice.

And did she ever! In 2008, Katy released a song called "I Kissed a Girl". The song was bold, catchy, and a little bit cheeky. Some people found it controversial because of its lyrics, but many more people loved it! It zoomed to the Number 1 spot on the music charts in many countries all over the world.

Suddenly, everyone was talking about Katy Perry! This song was like a firework itself, exploding onto the music scene and lighting up her path to stardom. After so many years of trying to find her place, this daring and unique song, combined with her emerging vibrant personality, was exactly what she needed to cut through the noise and get noticed.

"I Kissed a Girl" was the first single from her album One of the Boys, which also came out in 2008. This album was a huge success, selling millions of copies. It wasn't just a one-hit wonder;

it had other popular songs too, like the super catchy "Hot N Cold" (you might know the one where she sings about someone being "yes then no, in then out"!), "Thinking of You," and "Waking Up in Vegas".

With the success of her music, Katy's unique style also started to shine brightly. She became known for her quirky and vividly colored fashion choices. She loved to wear outfits that were playful and fun, sometimes inspired by pinup models from the 1940s, sparkly burlesque performers, or the super cute "kawaii" culture from Japan.

People started describing her style as playful and even "cartoonish" – in the best way possible! She wasn't afraid to be different and to express her personality through her clothes and her music. This bold and distinctive persona was a key part of her breakthrough, showing the world that Katy Perry was here to stay.

Fun Fact: Katy Perry's fans are called "KatyCats"! They got this nickname during her "Hello Katy Tour" back in 2009, and it has stuck ever since!.

Chapter 4:
Living the "Teenage Dream": Candy, Costumes, and Chart Hits!

After the exciting success of One of the Boys, Katy Perry was ready to show the world even more of her pop magic. In 2010, she released her next album, Teenage Dream, and it was a GIGANTIC hit!. This album was like a burst of sunshine and cotton candy, filled with songs that made you want to dance and sing along at the top of your lungs. It truly showcased Katy's powerful voice and her amazing talent for creating fun, unforgettable pop anthems.

Teenage Dream was packed with hit after hit! There was "California Gurls," a sunny song about California featuring rapper Snoop Dogg; the dreamy title track "Teenage Dream"; the inspiring anthem "Firework"; the out-of-this-world "E.T.," which featured Kanye West; and the super fun party song "Last Friday Night (T.G.I.F.)". These songs were everywhere – on the radio, in movies, and at parties!

Katy achieved something truly incredible with this album. She tied a record set by the King of Pop himself, Michael Jackson! She had FIVE Number 1 hit singles from the Teenage Dream album on the Billboard Hot 100 chart in the USA.

That's like getting five gold medals for one project! This amazing achievement showed that Katy Perry wasn't just a pop star; she was becoming a pop culture phenomenon, a true music legend in the making.

During the Teenage Dream era, Katy's iconic style fully blossomed. She became famous for what some people call her "camp" style – which means it was wonderfully exaggerated, playful, and theatrical. Her outfits were like something out of a fantasy world! She wore brightly colored clothes, candy-themed costumes (like bras that looked like they were made of whipped cream or cupcakes!), and outfits inspired by cartoons and Japanese "kawaii" cuteness.

Imagine concerts filled with giant lollipops, dancing gingerbread men, and Katy herself looking like a character from a magical candy land! This vibrant and imaginative visual identity was just as important as her music. It created a whole "Katy Perry" universe that was exciting and irresistible, especially for her younger fans, and made her shows and music videos incredibly fun to watch.

To give her fans a peek into her life on tour, Katy released a 3D concert documentary called Katy Perry: Part of Me in 2012. It showed the hard work, the fun, and the real person behind all the spectacular shows.

This era truly defined Katy Perry as a global superstar, influencing not just music but fashion and fan culture too.

Fun Fact: Katy Perry's Teenage Dream album was so popular, it had FIVE #1 hit songs! That's like getting a gold star five times for one project!.

Chapter 5: "Firework" and "Roar": Songs That Make You Shine!

Katy Perry has written many amazing songs, but two of them have become extra special anthems for people all over the world: "Firework" and "Roar." These songs are like musical hugs, reminding everyone to believe in themselves and to be brave.

First, let's talk about "Firework." This powerful song was on her Teenage Dream album, released in 2010. Katy herself said it was a very important song to her. "Firework" is all about self-empowerment, which means feeling strong and confident in who you are.

The lyrics encourage everyone to realize that they are special and have an inner light, just like a beautiful firework lighting up the night sky. You probably know the famous lines: "Baby, you're a firework / Come on, show 'em what you're worth / Make 'em go, 'Awe, awe, awe' as you shoot across the sky-y-y". The message is clear: don't be afraid to shine brightly!

The music video for "Firework" is just as inspiring.

It shows different people who are facing their own fears and insecurities – like a young boy whose parents are fighting, a shy girl who is nervous about her appearance, and a child in a hospital who has lost his hair. As they connect with the song's message, they start to glow and find the courage to overcome their challenges, igniting their own "fireworks" within. Interestingly, Katy said the song was partly inspired by a book called On the Road by Jack Kerouac.

Then there's "Roar," which came out in 2013 on her album Prism. This song is another super-strong anthem about finding your voice and standing up for yourself, especially after you've been made to feel small or quiet. Katy sings about going from feeling like she "stood for nothing" to finding her strength and declaring, "I am a champion, and you're gonna hear me roar!". The music video is also very cool – it shows Katy surviving a plane crash in a jungle and transforming from scared to strong, eventually becoming the brave queen of the jungle, even taming a tiger! It's a great picture of how someone can find their inner power.

These songs, "Firework" and "Roar," became so popular not just because they are catchy, but because their messages connect with people of all ages, including kids. They teach important lessons about self-acceptance, bravery, and having confidence in yourself. They remind us that everyone has something special inside them, and it's okay to be loud and proud about who you are. These songs have become more than just hits; they are cultural touchstones used to inspire courage. UNICEF even used "Roar" in a special video to inspire girls all around the world on the International Day of the Girl Child. That shows just how powerful music can be!

Fun Fact: The song "Firework" was inspired by a famous book called On the Road! Katy wanted it to be a song that made people feel proud and strong.

Chapter 6:
Beyond the Music: Smurfette, Super Bowls, and American Idol

Katy Perry is obviously an amazing singer and songwriter, but her talents don't stop there! She's also an actress, a spectacular performer, and a fun TV personality, showing that it's cool to try out different kinds of creative things.

Have you ever seen the movies about the little blue creatures called Smurfs? Well, Katy Perry was the voice of one of the most famous Smurfs – Smurfette! She lent her voice to this adorable character in the movies The Smurfs (2011) and The Smurfs 2 (2013). How cool is that, to bring a cartoon character to life with your voice?

Then, in 2015, Katy had one of the biggest honors any performer can dream of: she starred in the Super Bowl XLIX Halftime Show!. The Super Bowl is the biggest American football game of the year, and the halftime show is a massive concert watched by hundreds of millions of people all over the world. Katy's performance was unforgettable, filled with amazing costumes, giant puppets (including a very famous dancing shark that people still talk about!), and, of course, her hit songs.

Katy also shared her music knowledge and fun personality as a judge on the popular TV talent show American Idol. She was a judge from 2018 all the way to 2024. On the show, she was known for her bright and colorful outfits, her great sense of humor, and her encouraging words for the new singers who were dreaming of becoming stars, just like she once did. She helped them find their own voices.

And if that wasn't enough, Katy also had her very own spectacular show in Las Vegas called "Katy Perry: PLAY," which ran from 2021 to 2023. This wasn't just any concert; it was an incredibly imaginative and playful experience! Katy described it as "camp with a K" – meaning it was wonderfully over-the-top, fun, light-hearted, and sweet. The whole show was inspired by her daughter, Daisy, and the idea of seeing the world through a child's eyes. Imagine a stage filled with giant talking mushrooms, a dancing alarm clock, and other whimsical toy-like characters!. It was like stepping into the most amazing playroom ever!

These different adventures – from being Smurfette to rocking the Super Bowl, judging new talent, and creating a magical Vegas show – all show how versatile Katy Perry is. She's not just a singer; she's a true entertainer who loves to bring joy and wonder to people in many different ways, broadening her appeal to families and kids everywhere. Fun Fact: Katy Perry's Las Vegas show "PLAY" was like stepping into a giant toy box! It had huge talking mushrooms and dancing alarm clocks, inspired by her daughter Daisy!.

Chapter 7:
Katy's Heart: Family, Daisy, and Fun Hobbies!

Beyond the bright lights, catchy songs, and amazing costumes, Katy Perry has a life filled with love, family, and simple joys that make her happy.

One of the most important people in Katy's life is the actor Orlando Bloom. You might know him from movies like Pirates of the Caribbean or The Lord of the Rings. Katy and Orlando started dating back in 2016, and on Valentine's Day in 2019, Orlando asked Katy to marry him, and she said yes!. They share lots of happy moments and support each other through everything, showing that love and teamwork are important in any family.

The biggest joy in Katy's life arrived in August 2020, when she and Orlando welcomed their daughter, Daisy Dove Bloom!. Becoming a mom was a huge and wonderful change for Katy. She has said that Daisy is her "soulmate" and that Daisy "made me whole, and she healed me, and she showed me how to play again". Isn't that sweet? Motherhood has clearly been a deeply transformative and inspiring experience for Katy, influencing her happiness and even her creativity.

Daisy's name is very special too. Katy explained that "Daisy" means purity, "Dove" means peace, and "Bloom" (which is also Orlando's last name) feels like it means joy. So, her name is like "Pure, peace, and joy". Daisy is described as a fearless little girl with a strong will, and she already loves music, especially her mom's songs!. When Katy flew to space in 2025 (more on that later!), she even brought a real daisy flower with her as a special tribute to her daughter.

Katy also loves animals! She and Orlando adopted an adorable puppy named Buddy. She previously had another famous dog named Nugget,

who was so cute he was even nominated for an award for "Cutest Musician's Pet"!

When she's not performing or being a mom, Katy has some hobbies that help her relax. She enjoys cooking and gardening. Imagine her picking fresh vegetables from her garden to cook a yummy meal!

And, of course, Katy deeply values her fans, who she lovingly calls her "KatyCats". They have supported her throughout her amazing journey, and she always makes sure to show her appreciation for them.

All these parts of her life – her loving partner, her precious daughter, her pets, her hobbies, and her fans – make up the wonderful world of Katy Perry.

Fun Fact: Katy Perry loves her daughter Daisy so much, she calls Daisy her "best friend" and even took a real daisy flower with her all the way to SPACE!.

Chapter 8: Making a Difference: Katy's Big Heart for the World

Katy Perry doesn't just use her powerful voice to sing hit songs; she also uses it to speak up for others and make a positive difference in the world. She has a big heart and is involved in many important causes, especially those that help children and empower people. Her own experiences growing up with financial challenges seem to have given her a deep understanding and a strong desire to help those who might be struggling.

One of Katy's most significant roles is being a UNICEF Goodwill Ambassador. UNICEF is a part of the United Nations that works to help children all over the globe. Katy was appointed to this special role in 2013. Her main job is to help get young people involved in UNICEF's work, encouraging them to speak out about issues that affect them and to find solutions. She focuses especially on children who are very vulnerable – those living in extreme poverty, affected by violence or neglect, or caught in emergencies like wars or natural disasters.

To understand these issues better, Katy even traveled to Madagascar, a country in Africa, to see firsthand how UNICEF helps children with education and nutrition. She also generously donated a portion of the money from her Prismatic World Tour ticket sales to UNICEF. For all her amazing work, UNICEF honored her with the Audrey Hepburn Humanitarian Award in 2016.

Katy also started her own organization with her older sister, Angela, in 2018. It's called the Firework Foundation. This foundation is all about helping children from communities that don't have a lot of resources get access to the arts. They run programs like Camp Firework, where kids can participate in songwriting sessions, shoe design workshops, and choreography classes. Katy said she was inspired to start this because she remembers her own childhood and wants to give kids opportunities that she might not have had.

Besides these big commitments, Katy has supported many other important causes. She's an advocate for LGBTQ+ rights, animal welfare, breast cancer awareness (working with groups like the Young Survival Coalition and the Keep A Breast Foundation), and music education for kids (through charities like Little Kids Rock). She's also helped raise money for disaster relief, like for the victims of the Manchester Arena bombing and those affected by the California wildfires. She even partnered with the store Staples for a project called "Make Roar Happen," which donated $1 million to help teachers get supplies for their classrooms.

Katy's desire to create and support extends to her business ventures too!

- Katy Perry Collections: This is her very own shoe line, launched in 2017! The shoes are just as vibrant, fun, and unique as her stage costumes. In 2022, she took full ownership of the brand, showing her belief in herself and her creative vision.

- De Soi: Katy co-founded this company that makes sophisticated non-alcoholic drinks, which are like fancy, healthy beverages for people who want a special treat.

- Unsub Records: Showing her heart for new talent, Katy started her own record label in 2014. It's a way for her to discover and help new, emerging artists get their start in the music industry, just like others once helped her.

Through all these efforts, Katy Perry shows that being a superstar is about more than just fame; it's about using your platform to light up the world for others.

Chapter 9:
To Space and Beyond! Katy's Adventures in 2025!

Just when you think Katy Perry has done it all, she surprises everyone with even more exciting adventures! The year 2025 has been a big one for her, filled with new music, a spectacular tour, and an unbelievable trip... to space!

Katy is always creating. In September 2024, she released her latest album, titled 143. This album featured new songs like "Woman's World" and "Lifetimes," showing she's still making music for her KatyCats to enjoy.

Following her new music, Katy embarked on her "Lifetimes Tour" in 2025. The tour kicked off in Mexico in April, and she's scheduled to travel across the United States, then to Australia, Canada, and Europe, with the final show planned for Abu Dhabi in December 2025. This tour isn't just any concert series; it has a super imaginative theme! It's set in a video game world where Katy plays a character who is "half-human, half-machine." Her mission? To fight an all-powerful Artificial Intelligence (AI) called the "Mainframe" that has stolen all the world's butterflies!. She even wields a cool, glowing lightsaber-like weapon on stage during her battles.

This creative theme shows Katy is always finding new ways to entertain and engage with modern ideas that kids today love, like video games and AI. *

But the most out-of-this-world adventure for Katy in 2025 was her journey to SPACE! Yes, you read that right! On April 14, 2025, Katy Perry boarded Jeff Bezos's Blue Origin rocket, the NS-31 mission, and blasted off into space. And what made this trip even more special? It was an all-female crew!. This was a truly historic moment, showcasing the power and capability of women in exploration.

The flight itself was a quick one, lasting about 11 minutes. But in that short time, Katy and her crewmates traveled more than 62 miles (that's 100 kilometers!) straight up, crossing the Kármán line – the officially recognized boundary where Earth's atmosphere ends and outer space begins!. During those precious minutes, Katy experienced the amazing feeling of weightlessness, floating as if she were in a dream, and saw breathtaking views of our beautiful planet Earth from above. When she landed safely back on Earth, she was so moved by the experience that she kissed the ground!

And, in a sweet tribute to her daughter, she held up a daisy flower. Katy said the incredible journey made her feel "super connected to life" and "so connected to love," describing it as "supernatural". This daring trip truly positions Katy not just as an entertainer, but as a real-life adventurer and a part of space history!

Even with all this excitement, Katy still had time for a bit of fun with modern technology. For the second year in a row, AI-generated (meaning computer-made) fake photos of Katy attending a fancy fashion event called the Met Gala went viral online.

Instead of being annoyed, Katy posted the fake pictures on her Instagram herself! She joked that she couldn't actually be at the Met Gala because she was busy with her "Lifetimes Tour." And the funniest part? She said that this year, her mom wasn't fooled by the fake pictures because they were actually together when the photos appeared! (The year before, in 2024, the AI photos did trick her mom!). It's a funny story showing how Katy can laugh about the sometimes silly things that happen with new technology.

Chapter 10:
You're a Firework
Too!

What an incredible journey Katy Perry has had! From Katheryn Hudson, a young girl from a strict home in California with big dreams and a smuggled CD collection, she blossomed into Katy Perry, a global pop superstar. We've seen her sing her heart out in church, struggle to find her way in the music industry, and then burst onto the scene with unforgettable songs and a style all her own.

She's topped the charts with hit after hit, created magical candy-coated worlds on stage, and made us all feel like we could "Roar" with confidence.

She's lent her voice to a Smurf, dazzled millions at the Super Bowl, helped new singers find their wings on American Idol, and even zoomed into outer space on a rocket!

Katy's story is filled with so many inspiring lessons. One of the biggest is the importance of being yourself. With her quirky outfits, colorful hair, and bold songs, Katy has always shown the world that it's awesome to be unique and to let your true colors shine brightly.

Another huge lesson is the power of perseverance. Remember all those times record labels said "no" to her, or when her first album didn't sell?. She faced so many closed doors, but she never gave up on her dream. She kept trying, kept believing, and eventually, she got her big "yes!"

Katy's life also teaches us to dream big. Whether your dream is to be a singer, an artist, a scientist, an astronaut like Katy became for a day, or anything else you can imagine – no dream is too big if you're willing to work for it.

And perhaps the most important message from Katy, woven through songs like "Firework" and "Roar," is to believe in your own worth. Everyone has a special spark inside them, something that makes them unique and valuable. It's about finding that inner "firework" or your own powerful "roar" and not being afraid to share it with the world. Her songs often teach about self-acceptance and bravery, encouraging everyone to shine.

So, as you close this book, remember Katy Perry's amazing journey. Let it inspire you to find what makes YOU special,

And perhaps the most important message from Katy, woven through songs like "Firework" and "Roar," is to believe in your own worth. Everyone has a special spark inside them, something that makes them unique and valuable. It's about finding that inner "firework" or your own powerful "roar" and not being afraid to share it with the world. Her songs often teach about self-acceptance and bravery, encouraging everyone to shine.

So, as you close this book, remember Katy Perry's amazing journey. Let it inspire you to find what makes YOU special, to chase your passions with all your heart, and to never stop believing in yourself.

Because, just like Katy Perry sings, you're a firework too – ready to light up the sky!
Inspiring Quote: "If you're presenting yourself with confidence, you can pull off pretty much anything." – Katy Perry.

Printed in Dunstable, United Kingdom